20TH CENTURY MUSIC
40s & 50s
FROM WAR TO PEACE

20TH CENTURY MUSIC – '40s & '50s
was produced by

David West 👫 **Children's Books**
7 Princeton Court
55 Felsham Road
London SW15 1AZ

Picture Research: Carrie Haines
Designer: Rob Shone
Editor: James Pickering

First published in Great Britain in 2001 by
Heinemann Library, Halley Court, Jordan Hill,
Oxford OX2 8EJ, a division of Reed Educational and
Professional Publishing Limited.

OXFORD MELBOURNE AUCKLAND
JOHANNESBURG BLANTYRE GABORONE
IBADAN PORTSMOUTH (NH) USA CHICAGO

05 04 03 02 01
10 9 8 7 6 5 4 3 2 1

ISBN 0 431 14212 2 (HB)
ISBN 0 431 14219 X (PB)

British Library Cataloguing in Publication Data

Hayes, Malcolm
The 40s & 50s: from war to peace. - (20th century
music)
1. Music - 20th century - Juvenile literature
I. Title II. Nineteen hundred and forty-sixty
780.9'04

Printed and bound in Italy

PHOTO CREDITS :
Abbreviations: t-top, m-middle, b-bottom, r-right,
l-left.

Front cover m - (Michael Ochs Archive) Redferns,
br - Hulton Getty. 4-5t & b, 5br & 6tl, 6bl & br, 7r,
10b, 12tr & bl, 13br, 14m, 14-15t, 15br, 16 all, 17 all,
23bl & br, 24 both, 25 both - Lebrecht Collection. 3
& 29tr, 7tl, 18bl, 20bl & br, 20-21t, 26tr, 29mr
(Michael Ochs Archive), 4l & 22l, 18mr, 19bl
(William Gottlieb/Library of Congress), 8bl, 21tr (Max
Jones Files), 9tl (Glenn A. Baker), 29tl (S&G Press
Agency), 29bl (Chuck Stewart), 19tl, 19br, 21ml, 28tl
(David Redfern) - Redferns. 5tr & 11b, 9br, 10m, 10-
11t, 22-23t, 27t - The Kobal Collection. 8t, 11m -
Rodgers & Hammerstein Organisation/Lebrecht
Collection. 13tr, 27ml - Rex Features. 15tr, 26l, 27br -
Hulton Getty. 9tr - Kurt Weill Foundation/Lebrecht
Collection. 12br - Andre LeCoz/Lebrecht Collection.
14bl - Nigel Luckhurst/Lebrecht Collection. 23mr -
Royal Academy of Music/Lebrecht Collection.

*Front cover: Duke Ellington (main image),
Elvis Presley.*

*The dates in brackets after a person's name
give the years that he or she lived.*

*An explanation of difficult words can be
found in the glossary on page 30.*

20TH CENTURY MUSIC

40s & 50s

FROM WAR TO PEACE

Malcolm Hayes

Heinemann
LIBRARY

CONTENTS

FLYING THE FLAG
The Glenn Miller AAF (Army and Air Forces) Orchestra, with Miller himself on trombone, was sent from America to Britain in 1944. Their big band jazz sound went down well.

BERNSTEIN: A PHENOMENON
Leonard Bernstein (1918–90) was one of the most talented and versatile musicians that America has ever produced. He was equally at home conducting, playing the piano, and composing classical works or musicals.

'BIRD'
The new age of bebop found a superstar in Charlie Parker (1920–55). During his short life, he changed the face of jazz, as he explored new limits of technique and invention.

DISASTER AND RECOVERY

The devastation caused by the Second World War was so appalling that, even today, the world still feels its after-effects. The dropping of American atomic bombs on the Japanese cities of Hiroshima and Nagasaki introduced the most destructive weapon ever known to humankind. An uneasy peace followed, with constant tension between the two nuclear superpowers – the United States and the Soviet Union – and the nations that supported them. Classical music mirrored this new and uncertain world. There seemed to be no common language or set of values any more – what did the aggressive experiments of the European avant-garde have in common with the more conservative style of famous masters like England's Benjamin Britten and Russia's Dmitri Shostakovich? But this worried peacetime era did bring progress. In both America and Europe, jazz and rock developed and flourished, spurred on by the two musical symbols of the age: the long-playing record, and the electric guitar.

KELLY DANCES
Singin' in the Rain (1952) was the most famous triumph of dancer Gene Kelly (1912–96) in Hollywood's golden age of screen musicals.

WAR STORY
Shakespeare's play about the Battle of Agincourt (1415) was filmed in 1944, with music by William Walton (1902–83).

5

SIR LAURENCE OLIVIER'S
classic British film
hENRY V

By WILLIAM SHAKESPEARE

Sir Laurence Olivier
Robert Newton
Renee Asherson
Leo Genn
George Cole
Robert Helpmann
Leslie Banks

PROPAGANDA AND RESISTANCE

War affects everyone and everything, including a peaceful occupation like composing. The Second World War demanded that almost every major composer of the time should get involved. They found different ways of doing this.

CATCHING THE MOOD

In a world of aerial bombing, food rationing, and life-and-death struggle, people could at least cheer themselves up by going to the cinema. Films with a patriotic story were popular with audiences (who enjoyed them) and the authorities (who approved of them). In 1944, Laurence Olivier directed and starred in his film of Shakespeare's play *Henry V*, about England's victory at Agincourt in 1415. The film score by William Walton (1902–83) is one of the finest ever written.

HENRY V
Despite wartime difficulties, Laurence Olivier's film turned out to be as spectacular as Walton's music.

PATRIOT
Poulenc's wartime resistance was quiet, but determined. He refused to leave occupied France, and continued to compose there.

SHOSTAKOVICH THE FIREMAN
This picture of Shostakovich (left), almost certainly posed by the Soviet authorities, was taken during the siege of Leningrad.

GLENN MILLER

In 1944, England was full of American soldiers, preparing to invade German-occupied Europe. They needed to be entertained, and Glenn Miller (1904–44), as leader of the Army and Air Forces Orchestra, was judged ideal for this. His tunes, such as 'Moonlight Serenade' and 'In the Mood' were a huge success with English listeners, too. On 15 December 1944, Miller was on a plane to France. It disappeared, and has never been found.

Miller's plane was probably shot down.

A POINT OF HONOUR
Toscanini (1867–1957) refused to conduct in Germany or Italy while Hitler and Mussolini were in power.

RUSSIA RESISTS

Dmitri Shostakovich (1906–75) was in the Russian city of Leningrad when it was first besieged by the German army. We now know that the heroic resistance depicted in his epic *Leningrad Symphony* (1941) was about Soviet leader Stalin's savage oppression of his own people as well the siege itself. But at the time it caught the wartime spirit of nations pulling together.

When Arturo Toscanini conducted the western première on 20 July 1942, the live radio broadcast in the USA had an audience of 20 million.

PEACEFUL PROTEST

Composers in mainland Europe had to find a different way of resisting German Nazism or Italian Fascism. Living in hiding in Italy, Luigi Dallapiccola (1904–75) worked on his masterpiece, the one-act opera *Il Prigioniero* (The Prisoner, 1944–48) and his idyllic *Greek Lyrics* (1942–45). In German-occupied France, Francis Poulenc (1899–1963) wrote his defiant celebration of liberty, *Figure Humaine* (Human Face, 1943) for unaccompanied chorus. He insisted that it should not be performed until after his country was free once again. Both events happened in 1945.

STAGE MUSICALS

SAlthough America's cities were not being bombed and shelled as Europe's were, many American servicemen were casualties in the Pacific War against the Japanese, and in Europe too. Musicals helped to keep up morale.

RODGERS AND HAMMERSTEIN REWRITE THE RULES

Audiences on New York's Broadway liked musicals to be bittersweet stories of urban life.

This is the world of *Pal Joey* (1940), where composer Richard Rodgers (1902–79) and lyricist Lorenz Hart (1895–1943) came up with a classic song in 'Bewitched, Bothered and Bewildered'. But the stylized prairie setting of the wildly successful *Oklahoma!* (1943), composed by Rodgers to a book by Oscar Hammerstein II (1895–1960), was something new, and so was the way it drew together song, dance and drama. Rodgers and Hammerstein's other immortal creations included *Carousel* (1945), *South Pacific* (1949), *The King and I* (1951) and *The Sound of Music* (1959).

OKLAHOMA!
The great musical ran for 2,112 performances in New York, and for 1,458 when it came to London in 1947.

UNLIKELY LAWYER
Hoagy Carmichael (1899–1981) was still at law school when he wrote his immortal song 'Stardust'. His other hits included 'The Nearness of You' (1940).

8

IRVING BERLIN

More than 30 years after Irving Berlin (1888–1989) had made his name with 'Alexander's Ragtime Band', his way with words and music was still among the best ever. *Annie Get Your Gun* (1946) includes numbers like 'There's no Business like Show Business' and 'Anything You Can Do'. Berlin's last great score was *Call Me Madam* (1950).

Berlin wrote over 900 songs during his long life.

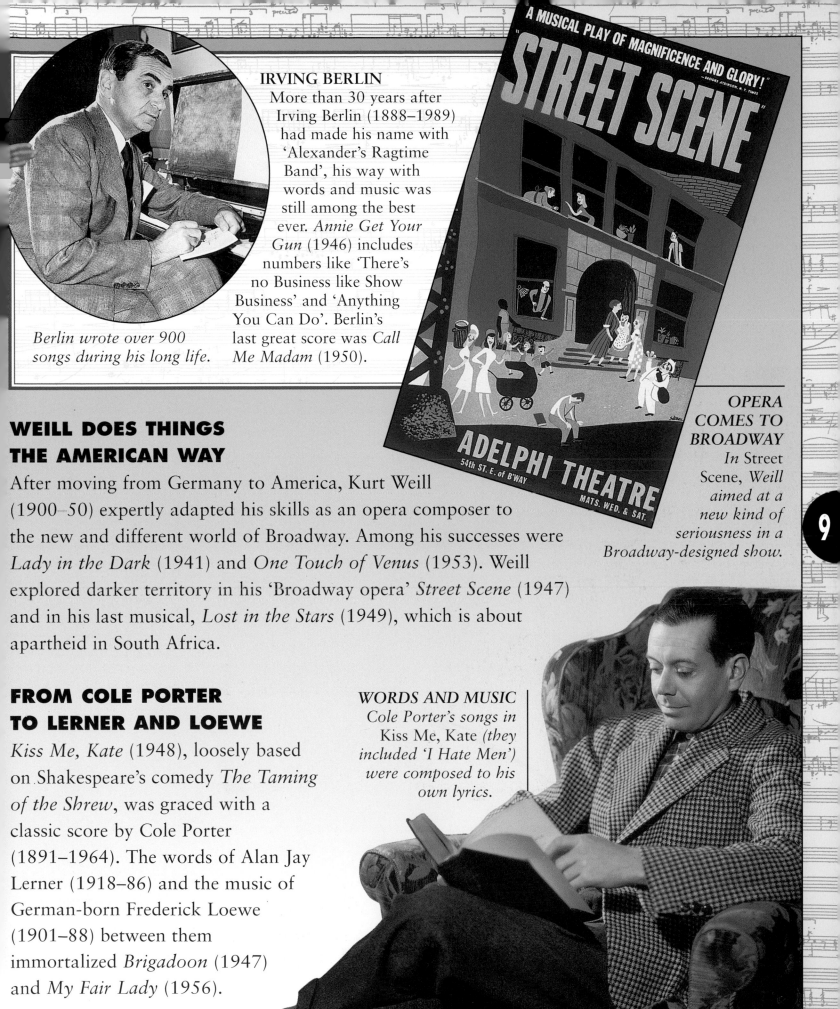

A MUSICAL PLAY OF MAGNIFICENCE AND GLORY!
— BROOKS ATKINSON, N.Y. TIMES

STREET SCENE

ADELPHI THEATRE
54th ST. E. of B'WAY
MATS. WED. & SAT.

WEILL DOES THINGS THE AMERICAN WAY

After moving from Germany to America, Kurt Weill (1900–50) expertly adapted his skills as an opera composer to the new and different world of Broadway. Among his successes were *Lady in the Dark* (1941) and *One Touch of Venus* (1953). Weill explored darker territory in his 'Broadway opera' *Street Scene* (1947) and in his last musical, *Lost in the Stars* (1949), which is about apartheid in South Africa.

OPERA COMES TO BROADWAY *In* Street Scene, *Weill aimed at a new kind of seriousness in a Broadway-designed show.*

9

FROM COLE PORTER TO LERNER AND LOEWE

Kiss Me, Kate (1948), loosely based on Shakespeare's comedy *The Taming of the Shrew*, was graced with a classic score by Cole Porter (1891–1964). The words of Alan Jay Lerner (1918–86) and the music of German-born Frederick Loewe (1901–88) between them immortalized *Brigadoon* (1947) and *My Fair Lady* (1956).

WORDS AND MUSIC *Cole Porter's songs in* Kiss Me, Kate *(they included 'I Hate Men') were composed to his own lyrics.*

MOVIE MUSICALS

Hollywood film studios decided that anything New York's Broadway theatres could do, they could do better. The golden age of screen musicals brought pleasure to millions all over the world, and still does today.

A CLASSIC IS REVIVED

Show Boat (1927), with its sparkling score by Jerome Kern (1885–1945) and lyrics by Oscar Hammerstein II, had already been filmed in 1929 and 1936. MGM studios came up with a sumptuous new version in 1951, starring Howard Keel and Ava Gardner. Rodgers and Hart's Pal Joey (1940) took on a new lease of life in Columbia's 1957 film, with Frank Sinatra, Rita Hayworth and Kim Novak.

TWO OF THE BEST

Irving Berlin's Annie Get Your Gun (1946), with Howard Keel and Betty Hutton, was released by MGM in 1950. Guys and Dolls (1950), with words and music by Frank Loesser (1910–69), had already been a Broadway hit. The 1955 film starred Marlon Brando, Frank Sinatra and Jean Simmons.

ANNIE GET YOUR GUN
Irving Berlin's songs included 'There's no Business like Show Business' and 'The Girl that I Marry'.

SOUTH PACIFIC
Released in 1958, the soundtrack of Rodgers and Hammerstein's musical topped America's LP charts for 31 weeks, and Britain's for 115.

10

RODGERS AND HAMMERSTEIN

Rodgers and Hammerstein's interest in portraying strong characters and unusual subject-matter gave the musical great depth and scope. This meant that their work transferred particularly well to the big screen. The spectacular results can be seen in *Oklahoma!* (1955), *The King and I* (1956), *South Pacific* (1958) and, later, *The Sound of Music* (1965).

Rodgers (left) and Hammerstein

HOLLYWOOD'S OWN CREATIONS

Some of the best-loved musicals were created for the big screen from the start. Bing Crosby had a huge hit with Irving Berlin's song 'White Christmas' in *Holiday Inn*, released by Paramount studios in 1942, but many of the greatest successes came from MGM. Gene Kelly starred with Fred Astaire and Judy Garland in *Easter Parade* (1948, songs by Berlin), and with Leslie Caron in *An American in Paris* (1951, music by George Gershwin, screenplay by Alan Jay Lerner). Kelly's greatest triumph was *Singin' in the Rain* (1952) with Debbie Reynolds. MGM's charming *Gigi* (1958), with songs by Lerner and Loewe, starred Leslie Caron and Maurice Chevalier.

SCREEN IMMORTALITY
Set in the 1920s, when silent movies were giving way to the new 'talkies', Singin' in the Rain deftly intercut its storyline with Arthur Freed's and Nacio Herb Brown's songs.

11

ENDINGS AND NEW BEGINNINGS

America offered a haven for European composers fleeing from Nazism and war. The new arrivals responded by enriching American music with their own longer and deeper classical tradition. Other European composers worked on while staying at home.

RELUCTANT EXILES

Austria's Arnold Schoenberg (1874–1951) had settled in Los Angeles. There he composed some late masterpieces including his String Trio (1945) and *A Survivor from Warsaw* (1947), whose text is an eyewitness account of Nazi ferocity towards the Jews in the Warsaw ghetto. Although Hungary's Béla Bartók (1881–1945) found life in New York difficult, he wrote his highly successful Concerto for Orchestra (1943) and Third Piano Concerto (1945). Germany's Paul Hindemith (1895–1963) composed busily while teaching at Yale University, before moving to Switzerland in 1953.

ONLY RECITAL THIS SEASON

Szigeti

Assisted by ENDRE PETRI at the Piano

Guest Artist
BENNY GOODMAN

Monday Evening JANUARY 9

First Performance Anywhere of
BÉLA BARTÓK'S RHAPSODY
FOR CLARINET, VIOLIN and PIANO
(Written for Benny Goodman and Joseph Szigeti)

CARNEGIE HALL

GOODMAN PLAYS BARTOK
The jazz clarinettist Benny Goodman impressed Bartók, who wrote his Contrasts *for him. Goodman and the violinist Josef Szigeti gave the première at New York's Carnegie Hall.*

GOING WEST
Hindemith's musical output in America included Symphonic Metamorphosis on Themes of Carl Maria von Weber *(1943) for orchestra, followed in 1946 by the choral* When Lilacs Last in the Dooryard Bloom'd.

BALANCHINE
The Russian-born choreographer George Balanchine founded the New York City Ballet, which staged Igor Stravinsky's ballet scores Orpheus *(1948) and* Agon *(1957).*

AN ENGLISH SYMPHONIST: VAUGHAN WILLIAMS

In wartime England, Ralph Vaughan Williams (1872–1958) produced his serene Fifth Symphony (1943). Then, in peacetime, still full of surprises in his old age, he composed the much bleaker Sixth Symphony (1947). Three more symphonies followed. In 1951 Vaughan Williams completed his masterpiece: the opera *The Pilgrim's Progress*, based on the story by the 16th-century writer John Bunyan.

STAYING PUT

Richard Strauss's (1864–1949) status as Germany's senior composer meant that he could live out the war at home without too much difficulty. His grief-laden *Metamorphosen* (Transformations, 1945) for string orchestra was his response to the destruction of Germany's opera houses by British and American bombing. Strauss's *Four Last Songs* (1948) were another late masterpiece. Austria's Anton von Webern (1883–1945) stayed at home, too, composing his two Cantatas (1940 and 1943). In 1945 he was accidentally shot dead by an American soldier in a mountain village.

STRAVINSKY CARRIES ON REGARDLESS

Igor Stravinsky (1882–1971) was born in Russia and lived for many years in France. So life in America (mostly in Beverly Hills, California) meant that he had, in effect, been exiled twice. Undaunted, he wrote a dazzling sequence of major works. These range from his opera *The Rake's Progress* (1951), which is still regularly staged today, to the ultra-concentrated *Requiem Canticles* (1966), whose serial technique was influenced by Schoenberg's and Webern's example.

Stravinsky eventually became an American citizen.

WORKING ALONE
Isolated in wartime Austria, where the Nazis had banned his music, Webern produced his last and greatest works.

OPERA REBORN

The arrival of peacetime conditions in 1945 meant that opera, the most complicated and expensive medium of classical music, became a realistic option once more. This rebirth of interest in opera was spurred on by the achievements of one brilliantly gifted composer above all.

Britten (left) accompanying Pears in a song recital

THE DAWN OF POST-WAR OPERA: PETER GRIMES

A committed pacifist, Benjamin Britten (1913–76) had left England for the USA (then a neutral country) in 1939. In 1942, he returned home and started work on his opera *Peter Grimes*. This is about a Suffolk fisherman, a misfit in his community, whose life is destroyed by intolerance and misfortune. *Peter Grimes* was premièred in 1945. Its great success made Britten world-famous, and single-handedly set in motion a post-war tradition of modern opera.

BRITTEN AND DUNCAN
Britten (right) and librettist (writer of an opera's words) Robert Duncan in the garden at Glyndebourne Festival Opera, looking at the score of The Rape of Lucretia.

THE TURN OF THE SCREW
Britten's opera, at once poignant and sinister, is based on a ghost story by the American writer Henry James (1843–1916).

BRITTEN AND PEARS
Besides *Peter Grimes* and many works for the concert hall, Britten also wrote two more large-scale operas, *Billy Budd* (1951) and *Gloriana* (1953), and others for smaller groups: *The Rape of Lucretia* (1946), *Albert Herring* (1947), *The Little Sweep* (1949) and *The Turn of the Screw* (1954). Almost all of these featured roles written for his partner, the tenor Peter Pears.

OTHER COMPOSERS JOIN IN

Two more English composers responded to the challenge of *Peter Grimes* in their different ways. Michael Tippett (1905–98) followed in 1952 with *The Midsummer Marriage*. In 1952, William Walton, living in Italy, completed *Troilus and Cressida,* set during the Trojan War in Ancient Greece. And in France, Francis Poulenc wrote an unusual masterpiece. His *Dialogues des Carmélites* (1957) is about the fate of a community of Carmelite nuns during the French Revolution.

TIPPETT
At a rehearsal of his oratorio A Child of Our Time *(1941), inspired by a young Czech's protest against Nazism.*

GERMAN NEWCOMER
Hans Werner Henze's originality quickly established him as a leading voice in post-war European music.

GERMAN OPERA REVIVES WITH HENZE

Germany's 200 opera houses needed a productive new composer, and Hans Werner Henze (born 1926) fluently set about meeting the demand. First came *Boulevard Solitude* (1952), an updated version of the *Manon Lescaut* story (used many years before by Italy's Giacomo Puccini). Henze's strange and colourful fairy-tale opera *König Hirsch* (King Stag, 1956) was then followed by the historical drama *Der Prinz von Homburg* (The Prince of Homburg, 1960).

RUSSIA AND EASTERN EUROPE

During the war with Germany and afterwards, Stalin and the Soviet Communist Party terrorized the lives of millions. Stalin's death in 1953 did not bring very much relief. Outwardly at least, composers still had to compose as the Soviet state demanded.

PROKOFIEV'S CINDERELLA

Prokofiev's (1891–1953) opera *War and Peace* (1943), based on Tolstoy's novel about Napoleon's invasion of Russia in 1812, caught Russia's patriotic wartime mood. So did his Fifth Symphony (1945), while his ballet *Cinderella* (1945) was also successful. But his much darker Sixth Symphony (1947) was officially disliked. Prokofiev died on 5 March 1953 – ironically, the same day as Stalin.

16

RUTHLESS RULER

Joseph Stalin had reinforced his grip on power as the Soviet Union's leader by ferociously suppressing any hint of opposition, either real or imagined. Musicians suffered like everyone else.

THE OFFICIAL PARTY LINE

Khrennikhov (left) composed many works conforming to the doctrine of 'Socialist realism'. He is seen here at a rehearsal with the conductor of Moscow's Bolshoi Opera, Boris Khaikin (1904–78).

KHRENNIKHOV SAYS: 'DO AS YOU'RE TOLD'

The Soviet Union's big idea for classical music was that it should be about 'Socialist realism'. Operas and ballets about the heroic deeds of Russian workers and peasants were acceptable, while anything that the Soviet authorities disliked was denounced as 'modernist' or 'formalist'. In 1948, Tikhon Khrennikhov (born 1913) became head of the Soviet Composers' Union and began an official crackdown. Shostakovich and Prokofiev were both denounced.

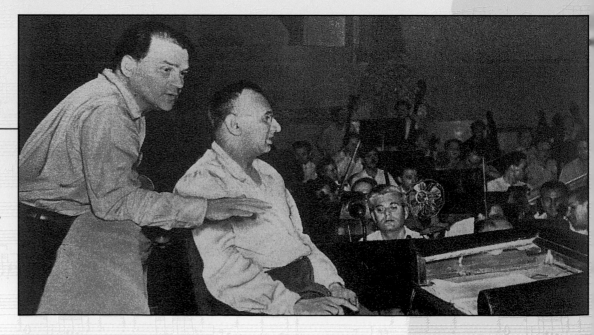

The Cinderella story has inspired many other composers, including Rossini (1792–1868).

KHACHATURIAN HAS FUN

Gayaneh (1942) was Khachaturian's other full-length ballet besides Spartacus. It contains the riotously entertaining 'Sabre Dance', which has since become a popular hit all over the world.

ULTIMATE MASTER

David Oistrakh (1908–74) was one of the great violinists of the century. He gave the first performance of Khachaturian's Violin Concerto, and Shostakovich dedicated his two concertos to him.

A VOICE FROM ARMENIA

Aram Khachaturian (1903–78) was one of the few composers of the Soviet empire who successfully balanced individual talent with the restrictions of official demands. His Violin Concerto (1940) drew brilliantly on the folk music of his Armenian heritage. And his colourful, passionately tuneful ballet *Spartacus* (1954) is about a slave who led a rebellion against Ancient Rome (a safely 'revolutionary' subject).

SHOSTAKOVICH PERSISTS, AND SURVIVES

Shostakovich was too famous and successful internationally to be silenced or sent to a labour camp, as millions of other Russians were. Even so, he wrote little apart from patriotic cantatas and chamber or piano music until Stalin's death. Shostakovich's Tenth Symphony (1953) brought him more or less back into official favour. He then reworked his First Violin Concerto (1948, revised 1955), and composed his Eleventh Symphony, subtitled *The Year 1905* (1957) and First Cello Concerto (1959). Between 1944 and 1960 he wrote the Second to Eighth of his 15 String Quartets.

JAZZ: FROM BIG BAND TO BEBOP

Bebop was the cutting edge of jazz in the 1940s. Despite its very different roots, it mirrored some aspects of modernism in classical music. Gifted soloists dominated; and bebop explored extremes of harmony, as classical 'atonality' had begun to 40 years earlier.

MASTER OF A NEW STYLE

Miles Davis (1926–91) was classically trained. He studied trumpet at New York's Juilliard School of Music, but soon gravitated to jazz, playing with Charlie Parker (1920–55) and Dizzy Gillespie (1917–93). As the wartime popularity of traditional big bands began to wane, bebop caught on. Davis's understated mastery on trumpet and flugelhorn – in a style often pigeonholed as 'cool' – became an admired alternative to Gillespie's over-the-top flamboyance.

MILES DAVIS
Davis fronted a band in the late 1950s, featuring John Coltrane and pianist Bill Evans. His album Kind of Blue (1959) *is often hailed as the greatest jazz record of all time.*

THELONIOUS MONK
Monk (1917–82) studied piano briefly at New York's classical Juilliard School. In the 1940s, he joined groups led by saxophonist Coleman Hawkins (1904–69) and Dizzy Gillespie. His music was so advanced that it confused many listeners.

CHARLIE PARKER
Known as 'Bird' or 'Yardbird', Charlie Parker was bebop's exploratory genius. He worked at various stages with Gillespie, Davis and Monk. Parker's composing and saxophone-playing – mostly on the alto instrument, rather than the more usual tenor – set entirely new standards of rhythmic and melodic invention. He is regarded as one of jazz's greatest ever soloists.

BEBOP'S FATHER-FIGURE

Dizzy Gillespie's trumpet-playing had already been a star feature in several big bands, including one led by pianist Earl Hines (1905–83), before bebop began to flourish in 1940s New York. Gillespie specialized in fantastic flights of virtuosity on a trumpet with its bell pointing upwards at an angle: when he tried out one of his instruments which had accidentally been bent, he found that his ear could pick up the notes more quickly. He was a strong supporter of rising younger talent, and collaborated with Miles Davis and trumpeter Clifford Brown (1930–56).

DIZZY GILLESPIE
Bebop made its real breakthrough with Gillespie's quintet, which included Charlie Parker, in the mid-1940s. Early audiences were bewildered by the new sound.

'TRANE': A DIFFERENT STYLE

John Coltrane (1926–67) made his name playing first with Gillespie, then with Miles Davis. He usually played tenor saxophone, sometimes also soprano and flute. 'Trane' (as the fans christened him) developed a style that blended vast virtuosity with a tougher, rasping tone which soon came to be known as 'hard bop'. In 1957, he played in a quartet with pianist Thelonious Monk.

Bird was given his nickname because he loved fried chicken!

JOHN COLTRANE
Coltrane started out on alto sax, but made his name playing the larger and deeper tenor instrument. The sounds he produced were unlike anything heard before.

JAZZ: ELLINGTON AND OTHERS

In jazz, as in classical music, the greatest artists have a way of still flourishing when their music has gone out of fashion. Duke Ellington (1899–1974) survived the decline of the big band era of the early 1940s in great style.

SYMPHONIC JAZZ

Working with composer and arranger Billy Strayhorn (1915–67), Ellington expanded jazz forms in a symphonic way, sometimes using a classical orchestra. In January 1943, his 48-minute *Black, Brown and Beige* was played at New York's Carnegie Hall. In the early 1950s Ellington kept to his larger band, although his immense gifts as pianist, arranger and composer could not stop his popularity dwindling. This suddenly changed on one legendary night at the 1956 Newport Jazz Festival, where the band's late-night session was a sensational success. For the rest of his life, Ellington triumphantly toured the world.

'PREZ'
Lester Young's mastery was so remarkable that Billie Holiday nicknamed him 'The President'.

20

GRAPPELLI AND REINHARDT

French violinist Stéphane Grappelli (1908–97) and Belgian guitarist Django Reinhardt (1910–53) together founded the Quintette du Hot Club de France. By the 1940s, its elegantly roguish performing style had become world-famous. The two then went their separate ways. After the Second World War, Reinhardt played briefly with Ellington in the USA before re-forming the Quintette, sometimes re-appearing with Grappelli.

Reinhardt (seated second from left) and Grappelli (right) with the Quintette

ELLINGTON
The 'Duke' and his band brilliantly kept the big band sound alive in the bebop era.

MINGUS
The virtuoso bassist first collaborated with Charlie Parker, Miles Davis, Ellington and others. Then he led a series of 'Jazz Workshop' bands, working with many different artists.

LADY SINGS THE BLUES
One of the greatest blues singers, Billie Holiday gave a legendary concert in New York's Carnegie Hall in 1948.

MINGUS: BASS-PLAYING TAKES OFF

Charles Mingus (1922–79) was one of jazz's great bass-players. Also a composer, he applied Ellington's idea of working with expanded forms to smaller groups – 'Open Letter to Duke' from *Mingus Ah Um* (1959) is his tribute to the great man. The bass's traditional function was to provide supple harmonic support to the other instruments, but Mingus's playing could also imitate the freedom of trumpet, saxophone and piano melodies.

TENOR SAX: DIFFERENT STYLES

Coleman Hawkins (1904–69) and Lester Young (1909–59) were not composers, but their contrasting styles of saxophone-playing had a big impact. Hawkins had a pungent, weighty sound that transferred well from big band to bebop. Young's playing was gentler and more reflective, and worked beautifully in tandem with the poignant blues-singing of Billie Holiday (1915–59). Ben Webster (1909–73) moved easily between rasping virtuosity and creamy lyricism.

21

BERNSTEIN AND COPLAND

The amazingly gifted Leonard Bernstein (1918–90) was a huge influence on America's musical life. He excelled as a composer of classical music, jazz and musicals. He was also a fluent pianist, and one of the finest conductors of his time.

BERNSTEIN: THE ALL-ROUND STAR

As a classical conductor, Bernstein replaced a sick colleague at a few hours' notice in 1943, and became famous overnight. Success soon came to his composing too. His Second Symphony (*The Age of Anxiety,* 1949) includes a brilliant piano part that Bernstein played himself at the première. He also wrote ballet scores (including *Fancy Free* in 1944), a violin Serenade (1954), and a one-act opera, *Trouble in Tahiti* (1952).

A MASTER OF MUSICALS

Jazz was a natural part of Bernstein's style, especially the bold, brassy sound of the big bands: his *Prelude, Fugue and Riffs* (1949) exists in separate versions for orchestra and jazz band. Jazz also colours Bernstein's musicals: *On the Town* (1944, filmed 1949), *Wonderful Town* (1953, filmed in 1955 as *My Sister Eileen*), *Candide* (1956), and the fabulously successful *West Side Story* (1957, filmed 1961).

LEONARD BERNSTEIN
When Bernstein was studying piano at Harvard, Copland encouraged him to compose his First Symphony (1942). Subtitled Jeremiah, *this was to be the first of Bernstein's several classical works on Jewish subjects. Soon afterwards came the musical,* On the Town *(1944).*

BERNSTEIN'S ON THE WATERFRONT

A grim story of dockside life and labour union corruption, Elia Kazan's *On the Waterfront* (1954) is one of the great films of the 1950s. It starred the young Marlon Brando, was showered with Oscars, and drew from Bernstein his only film score, which is remarkable for its strong atmosphere and driving energy.

Brando (right) won an Oscar for On the Waterfront, *though Bernstein missed out on an award.*

COPLAND

Besides Copland's popular ballet scores, his many other works include a Clarinet Concerto (1948), written for Benny Goodman, and Twelve Poems of Emily Dickinson *(1950).*

MUSIC FOR THE PEOPLE

Aaron Copland (1900–90) believed that classical music needed popular appeal as well as high seriousness. His *Fanfare for the Common Man* (1942) became the basis of his Third Symphony (1946). And while his opera *The Tender Land* (1952) has never had the success it deserves, his ballets *Rodeo* (1942) and *Appalachian Spring* (1944) were worldwide hits. His Piano Quartet (1950) uses aspects of Schoenberg's serial technique, but with different results.

COUNTRY BALLET

Copland's Appalachian Spring *was set in a pioneer village community in Pennsylvania. The story centres around a newly married young couple setting up home together.*

DANCE REVOLUTION

The original choreography of Appalachian Spring *was by Martha Graham. She became known as the High Priestess of Modern Dance, which she developed far beyond classical ballet.*

MESSIAEN AND THE AVANT-GARDE

Surrounded by cities destroyed by bombing, many of the younger generation of European composers were determined that modern music should break with a world which had brought about so much devastation. The mood was: 'New Music Starts Here'.

MESSIAEN SURVIVES, AND PROSPERS

Olivier Messiaen (1908–92) was captured by the German army in France in 1940. Imprisoned in a camp in Poland, he composed his *Quartet for the End of Time* in 1941, and played the piano in the first performance before an audience of 5,000 fellow-prisoners. Messiaen was repatriated to France in 1941. Some brilliant works followed, among them, in 1948, the spectacular, ten-movement *Turangalîla-symphonie*.

LONE SPIRIT
One of Messiaen's pupils was Jean Barraqué (1928–73), who fused avant-garde technique with the classical example of Beethoven. Barraqué's small but remarkable output included a Séquence (1950–55) for soprano and instruments.

MESSIAEN THE TEACHER WITH YVONNE LORIOD
Messiaen's classes at the Paris Conservatoire attracted many talented young musicians. Among them was the brilliant pianist Yvonne Loriod (born 1924), his future second wife.

Boulez (left) and Stockhausen (right) with Maderna in the 1950s

INTO UNKNOWN TERRITORY

Pierre Boulez and Karlheinz Stockhausen quickly became the dominant figures of the European avant-garde. But they were just two among many composers who saw their modernist movement as a journey of discovery together. Another fine composer, Bruno Maderna (1920–73), was also a gifted conductor, and gave the premières of many new works.

THE YOUNG LIONS

Messiaen also taught several of the leading young composers of the day, including France's Pierre Boulez (born 1925) and Germany's Karlheinz Stockhausen (born 1928). Boulez's chamber work *Le Marteau sans Maître* (1954) is a brilliant modern classic. Stockhausen worked on a larger scale in his ultra-complex *Gruppen* (Groups, 1955–57) for three orchestras. He also experimented with electronic sounds on tape in *Gesang der Jünglinge* (Song of the Youths, 1956). In Italy, Luigi Nono (1924–90) composed his choral work *Il Canto Sospeso* (The Suspended Song, 1956). This uses words by resistance fighters who had been executed in the war.

A TRUE ITALIAN
Like his country's opera composers, Luigi Nono wrote brilliantly for voices. His political stance inspired his choral work Epitaffio per Federico García Lorca *(1953), a memorial to the poet who was killed in the Spanish Civil War in 1936.*

25

AMERICAN RADICALS: VARESE AND CARTER

American composers were less interested in following the radical path explored before the war by Schoenberg and Webern. An exception was Elliott Carter (born 1908), who developed an expansive style of modernism in his First and Second String Quartets (1951 and 1959). Born in France, Edgar Varèse (1883–1965) became an American citizen. After a long creative silence he produced *Déserts* (1954) and *Poème Eléctronique* (1958), both using electronic tape.

STAR PERFORMERS

The rise of popular media – broadcasting, film, television, and above all the vinyl long-playing record (LP) – now meant that the musical stars of the age made composers and songwriters famous, rather than the other way round.

NELSON RIDDLE
The skill of Riddle's jazz-influenced arrangements was a major factor in Sinatra's vast success as a singer, although Riddle was always modest about his contribution to this.

26

A TRULY GREAT ENTERTAINER

Frank Sinatra (1915–98) began to make his name while singing with the Dorsey Brothers' band in the early 1940s. Within a few years he was a huge star as a soloist and film actor. His successes in musicals included Bernstein's *On the Town* (1949) and Frank Loesser's *Guys and Dolls* (1955). *Songs for Swingin' Lovers* (1956), with its canny arrangements by Nelson Riddle (1921–85), is one of Sinatra's many classic recordings. His unique style and ability to time a phrase meant that his appeal easily outlasted changes in musical fashion.

OL' BLUE EYES
The four-beats-to-a-bar style of swing, with its blend of easy charm and sharp rhythm, was Sinatra's natural territory. Working with Nelson Riddle and other arrangers, he recorded a whole sequence of legendary albums: Songs for Young Lovers, This is Sinatra, A Swingin' Affair, Come Fly With Me *and* Swing Easy!

FITZGERALD SINGS

Much of the popularity of Ella Fitzgerald's Songbook LPs was thanks to producer Norman Granz, who signed her to his Verve record label. She also recorded three albums with Louis Armstrong.

Bing Crosby (left), Dorothy Lamour and Bob Hope in the film The Road to Bali *(1952)*

BING CROSBY

Bing Crosby (1903–77) started out as a jazz singer of soaring talent, working with bandleaders Paul Whiteman (1890–1967) and Duke Ellington, among others. Moviegoers saw a rather different Crosby – the likeable crooner who starred in *Holiday Inn* (1942) and *Blue Skies* (1946), both with songs by Irving Berlin. *High Society* (1956), with songs by Cole Porter, was Crosby's only film appearance with Frank Sinatra.

ELLA FITZGERALD: AN IMMORTAL SINGER

The artistry of Ella Fitzgerald (1917–96) was on the same level as Sinatra's, although she was closer to being a true jazz singer, with a brilliant flair for 'scat'. From the early 1940s, she was the undisputed First Lady of American popular song. Fitzgerald's *Songbook* series of recordings contains performances of numbers by Gershwin, Berlin, Kern, Porter and Ellington which will probably never be surpassed.

LOUIS ARMSTRONG

Armstrong's huge success as a singer proved that in jazz, style can count for much more than true vocal quality. He's seen here on stage with Velma Middleton, in 1956.

ARMSTRONG CONQUERS THE WORLD

Louis Armstrong (1900–71) grew up in New Orleans, the original home of jazz. He became loved all over the world as 'Satchmo', the gravel-voiced singer and entertainer whom many consider also to be the finest jazz trumpeter ever. His 'scat' singing, too, was among the best. Armstrong's traditional style of playing was formed before the bebop era, but his popularity never waned during it.

ROCKING AROUND THE CLOCK

No one now seriously argues about when the age of rock 'n' roll truly began. In January 1956 Elvis Presley (1935–77) recorded 'Heartbreak Hotel'. No single recording in history has ever had a bigger impact.

PIONEERS
Bill Haley (centre) and his Comets paved the way for Presley's success with the classic 'Rock Around the Clock' (1955).

ELVIS: THE LEGEND BEGINS

Presley's gift was to blend a smouldering delivery more typical of a black singer with an instinctive appeal to the rebellious attitude of millions of white teenagers. His hard-nosed manager, Colonel Tom Parker, kept the hits rolling out, among them 'Hound Dog', and 'Don't be Cruel'. Next came screen musicals with title songs to match: *Love Me Tender, Loving You, Jailhouse Rock, King Creole*. Two years of US Army service in Germany then followed. Elvis now had a different, clean-cut image and a singing style closer to crooning. Critics accused him of becoming lazy with success. But his fans never stopped loving him.

ELVIS (MARK 2)
The 'King' emerged from army service without his sideburns, but with as much superstar appeal as before.

A SHORT BUT SWEET CAREER

Like Presley, Buddy Holly (1936–59) drew different influences together – such as rhythm and blues and teenage pop – into his own, very different style of rock 'n' roll. With his group The Crickets, he developed a fresh, breezy style of songwriting. Their best numbers, such as 'That'll Be the Day' and 'Peggy Sue' (both 1957), were huge hits before Holly died in an aeroplane crash.

CHUCK BERRY
Rock developed in America by blending several different styles, one of which was rhythm and blues. This had itself been propelled onwards from its blues ancestry by Howlin' Wolf (1910–76), Muddy Waters (1915–83) and Little Richard (born 1931). But it was Chuck Berry (born 1926), with his singer-songwriting talent and thunderous way with an electric guitar, who was the biggest influence on generations of rockers to come.

Berry's flamboyance on stage was a real crowd-pleaser.

BUDDY HOLLY AND THE CRICKETS
Holly (centre) was one of the first stars to use the hugely popular Fender Stratocaster guitar.

THE EVERLY BROTHERS SING TOGETHER

Don and Phil Everly started out with a style of pleasant, close-harmony duetting popular in the American South. But Presley's impact suddenly made this sound seem too tame. The brothers responded with 'Bye Bye Love' (1957), backed by a crisper rock 'n' roll beat, which quickly sold a million records.

OVER THE TOP
Little Richard pioneered something else: rock 'n' roll's trademark lyric 'Awop-bopaloo-bopa-wop-bam-boom!'

TALENTED TWOSOME
Don and Phil Everly became major stars with hits like 'Wake Up Little Susie' and 'All I Have to Do is Dream' (both 1957).

Glossary

AVANT-GARDE An artistic movement more challenging than conventional styles.

BIG BAND A large group of jazz musicians.

BLUES The original music of black Americans in the deep South, often mournful in spirit. Blues was part of the complex ancestry of jazz and rock.

CANTATA Italian for 'something sung'. A musical work using voices (as distinct from the instrumental 'sonata', something sounded).

CHAMBER MUSIC Music played by a group of solo players.

FLUGELHORN (from the German word for a 'winged horn'). A brass instrument with the full, rounded sound of a bugle, but with the keyed mechanism of the trumpet.

FUGUE A complex form of classical music where a melody is introduced, in sequence, in several 'parts' or melodic lines; these are then developed in parallel at the same time.

MODERNISM Used to describe music that sounds modern, when compared to what had come before.

PRELUDE Strictly, a piece of music acting as an introduction to others.

RHYTHM AND BLUES A style of popular music which originated in the 1950s, mixing features of the blues with lively rhythms.

RIFF A short, repeated, rhythmic phrase in jazz, and later in rock.

QUARTET/STRING QUARTET A work for four instruments; also the group that plays them. A string quartet consists of two violins, viola and cello.

SCAT An improvised vocal technique in jazz, using a stream of syllables (rather than actual words) as a way of imitating instruments.

SERIAL TECHNIQUE A way of ordering the notes in advanced, modernist music.

SYMPHONY Traditionally, an orchestral work in four movements, but it can be expanded to include extra movements and solo and choral voices.

TENOR A middling-high male singing voice. Also a particular size of saxophone.

WORLD EVENTS

- Hitler conquers France 1
- US enters the Second World War 1
- US Navy wins the Battle of Midway 1
- Fall of Mussolini in Italy 1
- D-Day – invasion of Europe 1
- End of Second World War 1
- First meeting of the United Nations 1
- India declares independence 1
- Apartheid becomes policy in South Africa 1
- People's Republic of China founded 1
- The Korean War begins 1
- First use of nuclear power 1
- America tests the first hydrogen bombs 1
- First ascent of Mt Everest 1
- US launches the first nuclear submarine 1
- Polio vaccine licensed for use 1
- Uprisings in Hungary and Poland 1
- Soviet Union launches a satellite 1
- First transatlantic passenger jet service 1
- Fidel Castro takes power in Cuba 1

TIMELINE

	MUSICAL EVENTS	THE ARTS	FAMOUS MUSICIANS	MUSICAL WORKS
0	Copland's Billy the Kid *first performed*	*The first Bugs Bunny cartoon films are made*	*Births of Beatles John Lennon and Ringo Starr*	*Britten's* Sinfonia da Requiem *for orchestra*
1	*Weill's musical* Lady in the Dark *staged*	*Release of film* The Maltese Falcon	*Birth of Bob Dylan, American singer*	*'Take the A Train' by Duke Ellington*
2	*Copland's ballet* Rodeo *staged*	*Humphrey Bogart stars in* Casablanca	*Death of Alexander von Zemlinsky, composer*	*Prokofiev composes Seventh Piano Sonata*
3	*Broadway première of musical* Oklahoma!	*Children's story* The Little Prince *published*	*Births of Mick Jagger and Keith Richards*	*Vaughan Williams finishes Fifth Symphony*
4	*Dizzy Gillespie joins Billy Eckstine's band*	*The Diary of Anne Frank is written*	*Glenn Miller's plane lost at sea*	*Copland's ballet* Appalachian Spring
5	*Britten's opera* Peter Grimes *premièred*	*George Orwell completes* Animal Farm	*Deaths of Bartók and Webern*	*Carousel, by Rodgers and Hammerstein*
6	*Release of musical* Annie Get Your Gun	*Release of film* It's a Wonderful Life	*Birth of José Carreras, Catalan tenor*	*Britten's opera* The Rape of Lucretia
7	*Thelonious Monk forms his first band*	*Laurence Olivier is awarded a knighthood*	*Birth of David Bowie, rock artist*	*Schoenberg composes* A Survivor from Warsaw
8	*Première of Cole Porter's* Kiss Me, Kate	*Release of John Huston film* Key Largo	*Birth of Pinchas Zukerman, violinist*	*Messiaen's* Turangalîla-symphonie
9	*Broadway musical* South Pacific *staged*	*Comedy film* Kind Hearts and Coronets	*Death of Richard Strauss*	*Weill composes* Lost in the Stars
0	Guys and Dolls *staged on Broadway*	*Akira Kurosawa directs Japanese film* Rashomon	*Birth of Stevie Wonder, American soul musician*	*Malcolm Arnold's first set of* English Dances
1	The King and I *staged on Broadway*	*Television show* I Love Lucy *first broadcast*	*Death of Artur Schnabel, pianist*	*Britten's opera* Billy Budd
2	*Release of film* Singin' in the Rain	*Film* From Here to Eternity *released*	*Birth of David Byrne in Dumbarton, Scotland*	*Tippett's opera* The Midsummer Marriage
3	*Shostakovich's Tenth Symphony premièred*	*Dylan Thomas's* Under Milk Wood *first heard*	*Death of English composer Arnold Bax*	*Weill's musical* One Touch of Venus
4	*Première of Walton's* Troilus and Cressida	*Novel* Lord of the Flies *by William Golding*	*Birth of Rickie Lee Jones, American singer*	*Boulez's* Le Marteau sans Maître
5	*Release of film* Oklahoma!	*James Dean stars in film* East of Eden	*Death of Charlie Parker, jazz musician*	*Stravinsky's* Canticum Sacrum
6	*Elvis Presley records 'Heartbreak Hotel'*	*Novel* The Fall *by Albert Camus*	*Death of Art Tatum, American jazz pianist*	*Messiaen's* Oiseaux Exotiques
7	*Boulez premières his Third Piano Sonata*	*Release of film* Bridge on the River Kwai	*Death of Sibelius*	*Bernstein's stage musical* West Side Story
8	*Start of the British LP chart*	*Publication of* Doctor Zhivago *in the West*	*Birth of Michael Jackson, rock artist*	*Luigi Nono's* Cori di Didone
9	*Ronnie Scott's jazz club opens in London*	*Billy Wilder's film* Some Like It Hot	*Buddy Holly dies in aeroplane crash*	*Elliott Carter's Second String Quartet*

INDEX